Penguins
and other Polar Animals

Printed in the U.S.A. • 1-40374-973-6
08 09 NGS 9 8 7 6 5 4 3 2

The Antarctic Region

The Continent

From outer space, Antarctica looks like a big "comma" of ice covering
5.5 million square miles. Most of the ice is about 6,500 feet thick!
This continent has plains, mountain ranges, and high peaks.

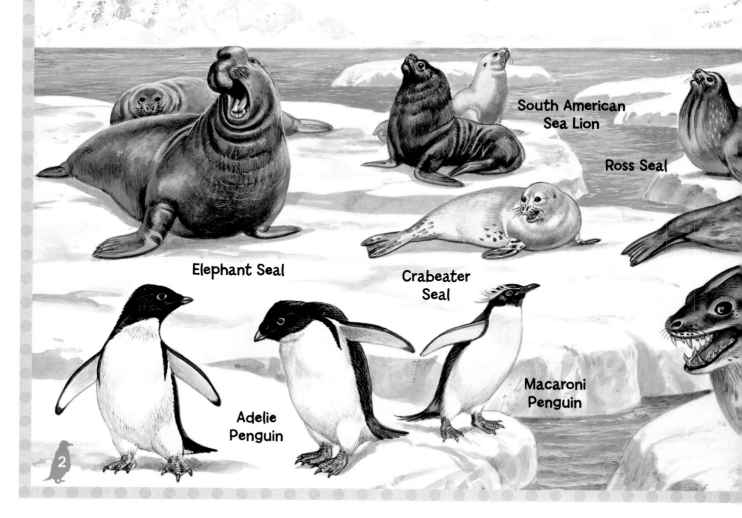

South American
Sea Lion

Ross Seal

Elephant Seal

Crabeater
Seal

Macaroni
Penguin

Adelie
Penguin

Wandering Albatross

Emperor Penguin

King Penguin

Weddell Seal

Leopard Seal

Antarctica has inland seas, small islands, and hundreds of miles of ocean dotted with floating land areas. Scientists think the Antarctic ice cap has 90% of all the ice in the world! The temperature stays mostly below zero but sometimes drops to −125° F!

The Ocean

Seawater freezes at 28.6° F. In winter, the ocean around Antarctica forms layers of "pack ice" up to ten feet thick.

The Animals

When currents lift up mineral salts from the ocean floor, algae called *diatoms* develop. Diatoms feed many animals living in Antarctica. Tiny shrimplike creatures, called *krill*, feed on the diatoms. Krill are then eaten by whales, seals, penguins, fish, and squid. Orcas and leopard seals are at the top of this food chain.

3

Emperor Penguin

The emperor penguin is the world's biggest penguin—up to four feet tall! It's covered with thick down and topped with glossy, black feathers. Like all penguins, the emperor has short wings, used to swim underwater. Emperor penguins can dive 200 feet and stay underwater for more than 15 minutes.

What does it eat?
Fish and small squid.

Did You Know?

If you tap a sleeping penguin's back, it won't notice—but if you touch its feet, the penguin wakes right up! Emperor penguins' feet are sensitive because they use them to hold eggs and chicks.

Baby Emperor Penguins

Emperor penguins nest far from the ocean. They join colonies during fall, and the female lays one egg. She gives it to her mate and goes back to the ocean.

The male takes care of the egg all winter. He huddles on the ice with other penguins, in the cold and dark, trying to keep warm. Then, at the end of winter, a chick hatches!

The mother returns with a belly full of fish, which she *regurgitates* (brings up from her belly) right into the chick's mouth. Then she holds the baby on her feet so the father can find his own food in the ocean.

Adelie Penguin

The Adelie penguin is a medium-sized penguin that nests in colonies close to the sea. Males come ashore to the same nesting ground in October and begin building a nest of stones. When the females arrive, they finish it together.

Baby Adelie Penguins

The female lays two eggs and goes to the ocean, while the male stays behind. After a month, the chicks hatch, and the parents take turns feeding them.

What does it eat?
Fish and small squid.

CREATURE FEATURE:
Adelie penguins were named after the wife of a French explorer in the 1830s.

King Penguin

King Penguin
Chinstrap Penguin

King Penguins are big penguins that nest in huge colonies.

The female lays an egg at the beginning of spring, and parents take turns *incubating* it (keeping it warm) for two months. When chicks are born, they are fed by having fish regurgitated directly into their mouths.

In winter, chicks huddle together for warmth. They eat every few weeks when their parents come to feed them. By springtime, they're grown!

Chinstrap Penguin

The chinstrap, smaller than the Adelie penguin, has nesting grounds near the Adelies'. Chinstraps arrive three weeks after their cousins, however, taking the places that Adelies thought were too rocky or rough.

These penguins are glossy black with bands of black feathers under their chins—like chinstraps! Their star-shaped pupils *contract* (get smaller) to protect their eyes from glare, and then *dilate* (grow larger) in the dark.

6

Magellanic Penguin

Magellanic Penguin
Macaroni &
Rockhopper Penguins

Magellanic penguin females lay two eggs that the parents take turns incubating. Then, while the male stays behind, the female goes to feed. When she comes back, she takes care of the eggs. Parents change places every two or three days.

Rockhopper Penguin

Rockhopper penguins nest on sheer cliffs high above the sea! They have bright yellow feathers on their heads and strong curved claws that help them climb rocks and hop—with necks outstretched, and flippers pointed back. Adults go to their nesting grounds to *molt* (shed feathers) in spring.

Macaroni Penguin

The macaroni penguin has a big beak, and an orange-yellow crest of feathers right in the middle of its forehead! ("Macaroni" was the name of a hairstyle in 18th-century England.) This penguin has a thin layer of down because it nests on subantarctic islands, where it's not as cold.

The mother lays two eggs in November, which the male and female penguins incubate for about 35 days. Chicks grow up by the end of summer.

African Penguin

African penguins live off the southern coast of Africa, and sometimes swim into the warm waters of Angola and Namibia. This little penguin has "tuxedo" coloring—a black back with a white belly!

Baby African Penguins

These seabirds raise their chicks on land. The female lays two eggs in a nest along the coast. She protects them from the sun with grass and leaves. Chicks hatch after about forty days.

What does it eat?
Deep-sea fish and mollusks (creatures in shells).

Galapagos Penguin

The Galapagos penguin, one of the world's smallest penguins, lives only on the Galapagos Islands. It's strange to find penguins at the equator!

Why are these penguins here? Because, many years ago, penguins swam in a cold current running up the coast of South America until they landed on the Galapagos Islands.

Baby Galapagos Penguins

These penguins nest between lava cracks in rocks. The female lays two eggs, but usually only one chick lives.

Did You Know?
Subantarctic penguins have one main predator—the leopard seal.

Leopard Seal

The leopard seal has a gray coat with black spots, and it can move fast with its long, bendable body. Unlike seals that sleep in the water (fatty blubber helps them to float!), the leopard seal snoozes on shore or hauls itself onto drifting ice.

The female leopard seal is ten feet long and weighs up to 1,100 pounds!

Baby Leopard Seals

Between November and January (Antarctic summer) the female gives birth to a pup that's about five feet long and weighs 65 pounds. She nurses her baby for two months.

What does it eat?
Fish and krill—but it's main food is penguins.

CREATURE FEATURE:
The leopard seal can open its mouth very wide. An elastic windpipe flattens to allow the seal to swallow huge mouthfuls!

Ross Seal

The Ross is the rarest Antarctic seal. It is small, with a gray-and-silver coat, a little head, and bulging eyes. This seal lives in the ocean, hanging out around pack ice and icebergs. It hunts in channels and climbs onto the ice to rest and breed.

Pups are born on drifting ice sheets, safe from enemies.

Did You Know?
Seals never drink water! Seawater is salty, so they get water from food.

Ross Seal

Crabeater Seal

Weddell Seal

10

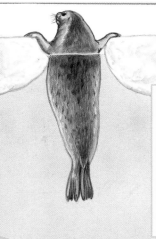

Weddell Seal

This seal, with its gray-and-white spotted coat, lives farthest south inside the Antarctic Circle. It loves to spend time in the water and lie in the sun.

Baby Weddell Seals

In spring, the female hauls herself onto the pack ice and has a pup. She nurses it yet doesn't need to eat anything—her fatty blubber is made into milk!

Crabeater Seal

The crabeater seal has a yellow-brown coat that is white in summer. It lives in small groups, fishing, sun-bathing, or just drifting on ice. And it watches out for *orcas* (killer whales)!

Baby Crabeater Seals

Crabeater seals form pairs for a whole summer. Mothers have babies on pack ice or floating sheets of ice.

What does it eat?
Mainly krill—not crabs!

11

Elephant Seal

There are two species of this seal: a southern one living in the Antarctic oceans, and a northern one in the North Pacific. Males weigh up to 8,000 pounds! Elephant seals roam the oceans, visiting the coasts of Africa, Australia, and Antarctica.

Baby Elephant Seals

In spring, the female has a black, woolly pup weighing about 90 pounds. With its mother's rich milk, the pup can grow to 330 pounds in a month! After nursing, it joins other pups on the beach to molt—and to get a waterproof gray coat.

What does it eat?
Squid, rays, and even sharks! In late summer, this seal doesn't eat until it has molted.

South American Sea Lion

The South American sea lion has a body covered with thick fur, and males have manes. Unlike seals, the sea lion has true ears and can turn its rear flippers forward to move faster.

Baby South American Sea Lions

In November, females gather on the beach. They each give birth to a pup with a soft, black coat. Soon the mother leaves and goes to the ocean to feed. She comes back to nurse her pup every few days.

Pups play while waiting. At three months, they're weaned and take to the ocean.

CREATURE FEATURE:
The sea lion's rear flippers have small claws used for scratching and grooming.

The Arctic Region

The North Pole is in the middle of the Arctic Ocean. A big area around the Pole is covered with floating ice that forms an icecap.

In winter, temperatures fall and ice grows over the sea and between the islands. This time of year, areas around the North Pole are dark for many months; and in summer, the sun never sets. As the temperature rises, the ice breaks, forming chunks called icebergs that are carried by the currents. (Icebergs are a great danger to ships!)

In summer, ice of the northernmost region thaws, allowing lichens, mosses, grasses, and low bushes to grow. This is called the *tundra*.

Life in the Arctic

Minerals from the Arctic sea-bed help algae grow. In summer, algae multiplies, becoming food for fish and *crustaceans* (animals with shells). The fish support birds, as well as different seals and walruses. Polar bears are the most important predators in this sea kingdom.

Polar Bear

Pomarine Jaeger

Arctic Tern

tiwake

Orca
(Killer Whale)

Walrus

Narwhal

Bearded Seal

Harp Seal

Hooded Seal

Harbor Seal

15

Polar Bear

CREATURE FEATURE:
Polar bears have been seen sleeping in the ocean during long crossings!

The polar bear is the largest land *carnivore* (flesh-eating mammal). In winter, an adult male can weigh 2,200 pounds!

This bear travels on pack ice, riding ocean currents and swimming in wide inlets. Sometimes the polar bear visits the continents around the North Pole. During the winter, it hunts. It finds shelter from blizzards in holes dug out of the snow.

Did You Know?

The polar bear's whitish fur is thick and water-repellant (doesn't soak up water). Thick layers of fat protect it from the biting cold and keep it afloat.

Baby Polar Bears

During winter only the pregnant female *hibernates* (sleeps in winter). She goes to a small den at the end of a tunnel, which she digs out of the snow on a mountainside, close to the sea.

In December or January, the female gives birth to one or two cubs. The newborns are very small. The mother polar bear curls up on one side and holds them on her belly, warming them with her breath.

In spring, the mother leaves the den with cubs that already weigh up to 35 pounds! The cubs stay with their mother for a couple of years while she protects them and teaches them how to hunt.

What does it eat?

Mainly seals. Sometimes walrus pups, rodents, and young musk oxen. When the ocean throws dead fish onto the beach, polar bears have a feast!

Walrus

Male walruses can weigh more than 3,500 pounds when their blubber is thickest. Their brownish skin is wrinkled and about an inch thick.

These *pinnipeds* (mammals with front flippers) are kept warm by a thick layer of blubber. They live in herds of about a hundred, and their main enemy is the orca.

Did You Know?

A walrus uses its ivory tusks—upper teeth that never stop growing—to heave itself onto the ice. It's called a "tooth-walker."

Baby Walruses

The female gives birth to a pup weighing about a hundred pounds and covered with short, gray hair. The newborn pup can swim. It follows its mother into the water soon after birth.

  The mother protects her pup by carrying it on her back when it's tired. She nurses it for more than a year, until its tusks have grown and it can feed alone.

What does it eat?
Mollusks, worms, crustaceans, and echinoderms (starfish and sea urchins) from the ocean floor. This animal can swim along the ocean floor at depths of 200 feet and stay underwater from five to ten minutes. Older walruses may also hunt young seals.

Harbor Seal

The harbor seal has smooth hair, from silver gray to almost black. It has a small tail and is clumsy on land—crawling like a caterpillar. But this seal is an expert in the water!

Big eyes help him to see fish even in poor light. In deep water, the habor seal swims belly-up to spot fish better.

Did You Know?

The harbor seal can stay underwater up to 45 minutes! Why? Its blood has many red cells that conserve oxygen, its heartbeat slows down, and its blood is redirected to the brain.

Baby Harbor Seals

In May or June, during low tide, the female gives birth to a pup in an uncovered area. Because the tide will return in about twelve hours, the pup sheds its "baby" fur while still inside the mother, and is born with a dark, waterproof coat.

When high tide arrives, the pup goes into the sea, floating with its mother for two days. When it learns to swim, the mother seal and pup go to a beach for nursing.

What does it eat?
Fish—up to eleven pounds a day! Also crabs and cockles, salmon and squid. Sometimes it just breaks into fishermen's nets for a quick meal.

Arctic Seals

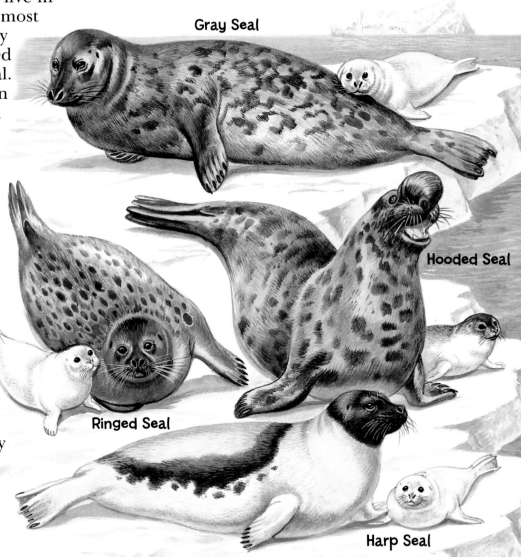

Gray Seal

Hooded Seal

Ringed Seal

Harp Seal

Many seal species live in the Arctic. The most common are the gray seal, harp seal, ringed seal, and hooded seal. They live in the open ocean and gather on drifting ice to rest, molt, and give birth.

These seals eat fish, as well as shrimp, crab, squid, and octopus. Some can dive 1,000 feet!

Baby Arctic Seals

Pups, born on the ice, are covered with thick white fur that hides them from enemies. At three weeks old, they molt, becoming the same color as adults.

Arctic Fox

The Arctic fox has shorter legs and ears than a red fox. Its layers of fat and thick fur keep it warm enough to survive the bitterly cold temperatures of the Arctic. Even the soles of this fox's paws are covered with fur, to protect it from ice and make sure it doesn't slip while running.

In winter, its fur is snowy white so it's invisible against the ice; in summer, its coat can be gray or brown, making it hard to be seen by predators (bears, wolverines, and eagles).

During the summer, this fox lives in the tundra, where it digs tunnels for shelter and safety. In the winter, it goes onto the pack ice.

Baby Arctic Foxes

The female gives birth to as many as eleven cubs between May and June. The mother nurses her cubs, but they are soon ready to eat whatever the parents bring them. At three months old, the young foxes are independent and leave their families.

What does it eat?

Mainly lemmings. Also plants, berries, and fruits, as well as the eggs of ground-nesting birds.

Lemming

The lemming is a small rodent with a spotted coat, small ears, and a short tail. It is *nocturnal* (active at night) and digs burrows to hide from enemies like the Arctic fox and snowy owl.

Lemmings eat grasses, mosses, and berries in the summer, as well as roots, shrubbery, and bark in the winter.

The female has up to twelve babies at a time. A few weeks after being born, little lemmings are on their own, and the female can mate again.

Arctic Hare

The Arctic hare has an all-white coat that stays white in summer. An Arctic hare's paws are covered with thick fur, which protects him from cold and helps him run faster over soft snow.

Young Arctic hares are furry when they're born and can already see. They run away right after they're born, and hide in the grass. Mother follows, to nurse them. After three weeks, little ones begin eating grasses and shoots.